CW00539971

'*Celtic Rhythms of Life* is a most welcome addition to the precious storehouse of prayer books drawing on the Celtic tradition… It is a practical and inspirational resource for both personal and communal use, diving deep into streams of ancient prayer and rooted robustly in the context of contemporary life.'

Ian Adams, poet, priest and photographer, and author of *Cave Refectory Road*

'Here are patterns of prayer for each day, to be revisited week by week, and long-loved by the dispersed and diverse Community of Aidan and Hilda. *Celtic Rhythms of Life* is flexible in its approach, inviting us to explore and reflect until the repeated words become familiar yet challenge us still more deeply. "May the Christ who loves with wounded heart open our hearts to love."'

Andy Raine, Northumbria Community

'All who wish to pattern our spiritual lives after the earliest Celtic saints' wisdom and faith will be blessed by this beautiful handbook of daily prayer, which brings the ancient Celtic tradition into our age with a dash of poetry and grace. '

Carl McColman, author of *Invitation to Celtic Wisdom* and *The New Big Book of Christian Mysticism*

'The authors have provided us with a wonderful worship resource. The liturgies are warm, original, creative, thoughtful and inspiring. Thank you!'

Revd Canon Michael Mitton, writer, spiritual director, speaker and canon emeritus of Derby Cathedral

 Ministries

15 The Chambers, Vineyard
Abingdon OX14 3FE
brf.org.uk

Bible Reading Fellowship is a charity (233280)
and company limited by guarantee (301324),
registered in England and Wales

ISBN 978 1 80039 229 8 (paperback) 978 1 80039 228 1 (hardback)
First published 2023
10 9 8 7 6 5 4 3 2 1 0
All rights reserved

Text © Graham Booth, David Cole, Simon Reed, Ray Simpson and Penny Warren 2023
This edition © Bible Reading Fellowship 2023
Cover illustrated by Rose Edwards, cover pattern © Almagami/stock.adobe.com

The authors assert the moral right to be identified as the authors of this work

Acknowledgements
Unless otherwise stated, scripture quotations are taken from New Revised Standard
Version Updated Edition. Copyright © 2021 National Council of Churches of Christ in
the United States of America. Used by permission. All rights reserved worldwide.

Unless otherwise stated, Psalm quotations are taken from The Holy Bible, New Living
Translation, copyright © 1996, 2004, 2007, 2013. Used by permission of Tyndale House
Publishers, Inc., Carol Stream, Illinois 60188. All rights reserved.

Scripture quotations marked MSG are taken from *The Message*, copyright © 1993,
1994, 1995, 1996, 2000, 2001, 2002 by Eugene H. Peterson. Used by permission of
NavPress. All rights reserved. Represented by Tyndale House Publishers, Inc.

Every effort has been made to trace and contact copyright owners for material used
in this resource. We apologise for any inadvertent omissions or errors, and would
ask those concerned to contact us so that full acknowledgement can be made in
the future.

A catalogue record for this book is available from the British Library

Printed and bound by CPI Group (UK) Ltd, Croydon CR0 4YY

Celtic

Rhythms of Life

Daily prayer from the Community
of Aidan and Hilda

Graham Booth,
David Cole, Simon Reed,
Ray Simpson and
Penny Warren

BRF
Ministries

With special thanks to Ray Simpson,
founding Guardian of the Community
of Aidan and Hilda, whose vision and
writings form the basis of these prayers.

Contents

TUESDAY: INCARNATION

WEDNESDAY: HOLY SPIRIT

THURSDAY: UNITY AND COMMUNITY

FRIDAY: THE CROSS

SATURDAY: THE KINGDOM

Introduction

To stay alive physically, we need to breathe. To stay alive spiritually, we need to pray. We pray in our own words, without words, or using the words of others. The Old Testament gives us the psalms; the New Testament gives us the Lord's Prayer; and after that we have the Spirit-inspired prayers of Christians down the ages. Praying words composed by others is not only biblical but it also helps us in so many ways: sometimes we cannot find the words to pray; sometimes others express things better than we can; and sometimes we need to be drawn out beyond our own personal concerns.

The Celtic Christians of the first millennium have often been a great source of inspiration. This vibrant expression of Christianity planted the good news of Jesus across the British Isles and beyond. It somehow wove together a Catholic spirituality of sacrament and incarnation, an Evangelical spirituality of scripture and mission, a Pentecostal-charismatic spirituality of the presence and power of God, an Orthodox spirituality of the Trinity, time and eternity, a closeness to the natural world and a robust commitment to social justice. Daily rhythms of prayer were at the heart of this movement of God. Centuries later, a different expression of Celtic spirituality lived on in the prayers of the Hebridean islanders collected by Alexander Carmichael in the *Carmina Gadelica*. These prayers weave together the unseen world and everyday life in simple, vivid poetry. They join hard hands and warm hearts.

For over 25 years the international Community of Aidan and Hilda (**aidanandhilda.org.uk**) has been reconnecting with this Celtic spiritual heritage and seeking to re-express it for today. A daily rhythm of prayer is one of the foundations of our community life. Ray Simpson, one of the Community's founders, has written widely on Celtic spirituality and is the author of many prayer resources. Over time, the Community has revised and added to this material, resulting in this new publication providing four daily prayer stops for the seven days of the week. These prayer patterns contain material written and compiled by Graham Booth, Brother Cassian (David Cole), Simon Reed, Ray Simpson and Penny Warren, with help from Alison Price in compiling the Bible readings.

Our hope is that this book helps breathe the life of God afresh into your prayers, and that as we pray together we reconnect the Spirit and the scriptures, the saints and the streets, the seasons and the soil.

How to use this book

- There are four prayer stops each day (morning, midday, evening and night). Use as many as are right for you. Building a regular pattern helps, but don't worry if you miss one.

- The prayer patterns are laid out for more than one voice, but they work just as well on your own.

- For morning and evening prayer, there is a choice of four psalms (one of them printed in the text) and four Bible readings from both the Old and the New Testament. These may be used in any combination or followed as a monthly cycle. The psalms and readings are linked to the theme of the day, but any other psalms or reading scheme may be used instead.

- Each day has its own theme:

  - Sunday: resurrection

  - Monday: creation

  - Tuesday: incarnation

  - Wednesday: Holy Spirit

  - Thursday: unity and community

  - Friday: the cross

  - Saturday: the kingdom

- In special seasons you might like to use the same theme every day, e.g. Sunday/resurrection during Easter, Tuesday/incarnation during Christmas or Friday/the cross during Lent or Holy Week, if you observe this.

- Praying the psalms is an ancient Jewish/Christian practice. Sometimes they express exactly what we are feeling, but not always. It can be helpful to imagine that we are praying on behalf of others who are in a different situation. Instead of just reading a psalm, we could try alternating voices (if in a group), pausing briefly between verses or pausing briefly in the middle of each verse.

- What happens between the words is as important as what we say. Feel free to leave spaces, miss things out or add things in, if that is how the Spirit seems to be leading you.

- In churches with a liturgical tradition, these prayer patterns may be used in Daily Prayer. In the Church of England, the inclusion of a collect and the Lord's Prayer is all that is required.

Acknowledgements

All psalms are taken from the New Living Translation (NLT) of the Bible or paraphrased by Ray Simpson, apart from Tuesday evening prayer and Thursday morning prayer from the *USA Book Of Common Prayer*.

All Bible readings are taken from the New Revised Standard Version (NRSV), unless otherwise noted, or paraphrased by the authors of this book.

Simon Reed

Sunday

morning prayer

Rising from death, today Christ greets his people.
**Rising with all creation, we greet you as
our King.**

There may be singing.

Either
Psalm 24 is said as follows:

The earth is the Lord's, and everything in it.
The world and all its people belong to him.

**For he laid the earth's foundation on the seas
and built it on the ocean depths.**

Who may climb the mountain of the Lord?
Who may stand in his holy place?

Only those whose hands and hearts are pure,
who do not worship idols
and never tell lies.

They will receive the Lord's blessing
and have a right relationship with God
    their Saviour.

Such people may seek you
and worship in your presence, O God of Jacob.

Open up, ancient gates!
Open up, ancient doors,
and let the King of glory enter.

Who is the King of glory?
The Lord, strong and mighty;
the Lord, invincible in battle.

Open up, ancient gates!
Open up, ancient doors,
and let the King of glory enter.

Who is the King of glory?
The Lord of Heaven's Armies –
he is the King of glory.

Or
Psalm 57, Psalm 95:1–7, Psalm 100 or the psalm of
the day from a lectionary or reading scheme; or any
other psalm.

Let us recollect the presence of the risen Christ
with us now.

Short silence.

Christ Jesus, in the light of your risen presence,
and in union with your first frail apostles,
we say sorry for the times when we have failed to
follow you:
for not weighing your words,
for not sharing your trials,
for not believing your promises.

Things for which we are sorry may be recalled aloud
or in silence.

Risen Christ, disperse the sin from our souls as
the mist departs from the hills.
Be in what we do, inform what we say, redeem
who we are. Amen.

*Isaiah 25:6–9, Isaiah 35:1–10, Hosea 6:1–6, Micah
6:6–8 or the reading of the day from a lectionary or
reading scheme; or another Old Testament reading.*

There may be singing, silence or the following:

> We believe, O God of all gods,
> that you are the eternal God of life.
> **We believe, O God of all peoples,**
> **that you are the eternal God of love.**
> We believe that you create earth and seas
>   and skies,
> **we believe that you create us in your image**
> **and give us eternal worth.**

*Luke 24:1–12, Philippians 3:7–16, Colossians 3:12–17,
Revelation 1:12–20 or the reading of the day from
a lectionary or reading scheme; or another New
Testament reading.*

> Jesus says:
> I am the resurrection and the life.
> **You break the power of sin and death.**
> I am the bread of life.
> **You feed and fill the hungry.**
> I am the true vine.
> **You make empty lives bear fruit.**

There may be silence or singing.

Either
Use the following set of prayers, pausing after each to invite the risen Christ into specific situations, perhaps visualising his response.

Risen Christ,
you appeared to Mary in the garden at dawn;
**Make yourself known to us in the dawnings of
    our lives.**

You appeared to the fishermen as they toiled
    in vain;
**Make yourself known to us in the long hours of
    our weekly work.**

You appeared to the walkers as they welcomed
    you to their table;
**Make yourself known to us in our life's journey
    and make welcoming our homes.**

You appeared to Thomas when he touched the
    scars in your body;
**Make yourself known when we touch the
    wounds of the world.**

You appeared to many as they met beneath
the skies;
**Make yourself known to us in the wonder of
your creation.**

Or
*Use the following set of prayers in which each of the
themes may be used as a starting point for more
extended intercessions.*

We pray for believers;
may their lives be signs of joyful service.

We pray that our churches may bring honour
to you;
and healing to the people.

We pray for people in authority;
may they strive for justice and peace.

We pray for our communities;
may refreshment be found by all who work.

We pray for our homes;
may they be places of hospitality and hope.

There may be singing or the Lord's Prayer.

The Father of life go with us.
The risen Christ beside us.
The vibrant Spirit within us.

Sunday

midday prayer

Alleluia. Christ is risen.
Alleluia. Christ is risen.

Either
Psalm 30:1–5 is said as follows.

I will exalt you, Lord, for you rescued me,
You refused to let my enemies triumph over me.

O Lord my God, I cried to you for help,
and you restored my health.

You brought me up from the grave, O Lord.
You kept me from falling into the pit of death.

Sing to the Lord, all you godly ones!
Praise his holy name.

For his anger lasts only a moment,
but his favor lasts a lifetime!

**Weeping may last through the night,
but joy comes with the morning.**

Or
Alleluias may be sung.

We welcome your presence in the midst of
    the day;
**a day for rest and renewal,
a day for worship and well-being
a day for sharing food and friendship.**

A candle may be lit.

Before food one of the following prayers may be said.

Either

I would prepare a feast
and be host to the great High King,
with all the company of heaven.
The nourishment of pure love be in my house,
and the roots of repentance.

May we have baskets of love to give,
with cups of mercy for everybody.
Sweet Jesus, be here for us,
with all the company of heaven.
May this meal be full of cheerfulness,
for this is a feast of the great High King,
who is our host for all eternity.[1]

Or

May the abundance and joy of creation be with
us as we eat.
May the abundance and joy of Christ be with us
as we meet.

Or

The food which we are to eat
is earth, water and sun,
coming to us through pleasing plants.
The food which we are to eat
is the fruit of much labour.
We are thankful for it.
May it give us health, strength and joy,
and may it increase our love.

Risen Christ of the miraculous catching of fish
and the perfect lakeside meal,
be with us as we share this meal.

Generous God, as once you multiplied the five
    loaves and two fishes,
multiply the gifts each of us brings
that from our sharing together blessings
    may flow.

I know what it is to have little, and I know what
it is to have plenty. In any and all circumstances
I have learned the secret of being well-fed and
of going hungry, of having plenty and of being
in need. I can do all things through him who
strengthens me.
PHILIPPIANS 4:12–13

There may be meditation and singing.

Rejoicing in your new creation,
let us pray as you have taught us.

The Lord's Prayer.

Keep us in the beautiful attitudes,
simple, joyful and gentle.

Let us bless the Lord.
Thanks be to God.

Sunday

evening prayer

Spirit of the risen Christ,
as the lamps light up the evening,
shine into our hearts and kindle in us the fire of
your love.

A candle may be lit.

Jesus Christ is the light of world;
a light that no darkness can quench.

The long reign of sin has ended.
A new age has dawned.
A broken world is being renewed.
and we are once again made whole.
Alleluia!

There may be singing.

Either
Psalm 92 is said as follows.

It is good to give thanks to the Lord,
to sing praises to the Most High.
It is good to proclaim your unfailing love in
    the morning,
your faithfulness in the evening,
accompanied by a ten-stringed instrument,
    a harp and the melody of a lyre.

**You thrill me, Lord, with all you have done
    for me!
I sing for joy because of what you have done.
O Lord, what great works you do!
And how deep are your thoughts.**

Only a simpleton would not know,
and only a fool would not understand this:
Though the wicked sprout like weeds
and evildoers flourish,
they will be destroyed forever.
But you, O Lord, will be exalted forever.
Your enemies, Lord, will surely perish;
all evildoers will be scattered.

But you have made me as strong as a wild ox.
You have anointed me with the finest oil.
My eyes have seen the downfall of my enemies;
my ears have heard the defeat of my
**   wicked opponents.**

But the godly will flourish like palm trees
and grow strong like the cedars of Lebanon.
For they are transplanted to the Lord's
    own house.
They flourish in the courts of our God.
Even in old age they will still produce fruit;
they will remain vital and green.

They will declare, 'The Lord is just!
He is my rock! There is no evil in him!'

Or
Psalm 27, Psalm 84, Psalm 138 or the psalm of the day
from a lectionary or reading scheme; or any other psalm.

We offer to you, Lord, the concerns of this day;
we lay down our burdens at your feet.

Short silence.

Forgive us our sins, give us your peace
and help us to receive your word.
In the name of Christ. Amen.

*Exodus 3:1–15, Isaiah 55:1–13, Ezekiel 47:1–12,
Zechariah 10:6–12, or the reading of the day from
a lectionary or reading scheme; or another Old
Testament reading.*

There may be singing, silence or the following:

Risen Christ, you turned Mary's tears into joy:
turn our tears into joy.
Risen Christ, you turned the travellers' despair
into hope:
turn our despair into hope.
Risen Christ, you turned the disciples' fears
into boldness;
turn our fears into boldness.
Risen Christ, you turned Thomas' unbelief
into trust:
turn our unbelief into trust.

*John 20:1–18, 1 Corinthians 15:20–28, Hebrews
4:1–11, 1 Peter 1:3–9 or the reading of the day from
a lectionary or reading scheme; or another New
Testament reading.*

Silent reflection, teaching or singing, or the Magnificat
(Song of Mary) may be said as follows:

My soul proclaims the greatness of the Lord,
my spirit rejoices in God my Saviour;
he has looked with favour on his lowly servant.

**From this day all generations will call
    me blessed;
the Almighty has done great things for me
    and holy is his name.**

He has mercy on those who fear him, from
    generation to generation.

**He has shown strength with his arm
and has scattered the proud in their conceit,**

Casting down the mighty from their thrones
and lifting up the lowly.

**He has filled the hungry with good things
and sent the rich away empty.**

He has come to the aid of his servant Israel,
to remember his promise of mercy,

the promise made to our ancestors,
to Abraham and his children forever.

Continue:

We give you thanks, our Provider, that you are
always present, in all things, each day and
each night.
We give you thanks for your gifts of creation,
life and friendship.
We give you thanks for the particular blessings
of this day.

Blessings may be named in silence or aloud.

*Specific people or situations may be named in each
prayer.*

Risen Christ, into your hands we place our
families, our neighbours, our fellow believers,
and all with whom we have connected today.

Risen Christ,
enfold them in your will.

Risen Christ, into your hands we place all who are
victims of prejudice, oppression or neglect;
the frail, the unwanted.

Risen Christ,
**may everyone be cherished from conception to
the grave.**

Risen Christ, into your hands we place all who are
restless, sick or prey to the powers of evil.

Risen Christ,
tenderly watch over and care for them.

Risen Christ, bring renewal to the land and to
the church; to ordained ministries and to
religious communities.

Risen Christ,
**raise up new callings and communities that
meet the needs of our times.**

There may be singing or the Lord's Prayer.

Lord Jesus Christ, light of the world,
by your cross you have overcome all darkness
   that oppresses.
**Come and shine on us here, that we may grow
   and live together in your love which makes
   us one with all humanity.**

**The grace of our Lord Jesus Christ,
the love of God,
and the fellowship of the Holy Spirit
be with us all evermore. Amen.**

Sunday

night prayer

Risen Saviour,
as we settle to rest this night,
we rest in the knowledge of your victory
    over darkness.

Lighten our darkness,
as a full moon brightens the darkness of night.
Lighten our darkness,
as the stars shine in the clear night sky.
Lighten our darkness,
and bring us peace this night.

Psalm 16 is said as follows.

Keep me safe, O God,
for I have come to you for refuge.

I said to the Lord, 'You are my Master!
Every good thing I have comes from you.'

The godly people in the land are my true heroes!
I take pleasure in them!

**Troubles multiply for those who chase after
     other gods.**
I will not take part in their sacrifices of blood
or even speak the names of their gods.

Lord, you alone are my inheritance,
my cup of blessing.
You guard all that is mine.

The land you have given me is a pleasant land.
What a wonderful inheritance!

I will bless the Lord who guides me;
even at night my heart instructs me.

I know the Lord is always with me.
I will not be shaken, for he is right beside me.

No wonder my heart is glad, and I rejoice.
My body rests in safety.
For you will not leave my soul among the dead
or allow your holy one to rot in the grave.

**You will show me the way of life,
granting me the joy of your presence
and the pleasures of living with you forever.**

Continue:

> May that part of me that did not grow at morning,
> grow at nightfall.

Pause.

> The light of Christ shines upon us this night,
> driving all darkness from our hearts, our
> minds, our souls.
> **The light of Christ shines upon us this night,
> bringing the divine presence with its
> glorious beams.**

1 John 1:1–5 is read.

> We declare to you what was from the beginning,
> what we have heard, what we have seen with our
> eyes, what we have looked at and touched with
> our hands, concerning the word of life – this life
> was revealed, and we have seen it and testify to
> it, and declare to you the eternal life that was

with the Father and was revealed to us – what
we have seen and heard we also declare to you
so that you also may have fellowship with us,
and truly our fellowship is with the Father and
with his Son Jesus Christ. We are writing these
things so that our joy may be complete. This
is the message we have heard from him and
proclaim to you, that God is light and in him
there is no darkness at all.

There may be singing, or open or silent prayer.

Risen Christ,
shine upon me this night
that your glory will guide me, lead me, hold me.
Shine upon me this night
that I will be made new.
Shine upon me this night
that others will see you shining from me
as I rise tomorrow.

We end this day knowing Christ's rising,
the end of the reign of darkness
in our world, in our hearts and in our minds.
May divine light bathe us in glory and enfold us
    in love.

Monday

morning prayer

God of life, you summon the day to dawn
and call us to create with you.

You are the Rock from whom all earth is formed.
You are the Food from whom all souls are fed.
You are the Force from whom all powers flow.
You are the Source who is creation's head.

There may be singing.

Either
Verses from Psalm 104 are said by alternating voices.

First
    Creator God, how great you are!
    You clothe yourself in light;
    you stretch out the skies like a tent.

Second

    Winds are your messengers,
    flames are your servants.
    You water the earth until it gives us food.

First

    How abundant are your works, O God,
    in wisdom have you made them all.

Second

    The creatures teeming the earth,
    the sea, vast and wide –
    innumerable things, small and great,
        live within it.

**All these look to you for their food in
    due season.
When you send forth your Spirit they
    are created
and you renew the face of the earth.**

First

    May your glory last forever,
    may you always have joy in what you
        have created.

Second

May our thoughts always give you pleasure,
may we always rejoice in you.[2]

Continue:

Glory to you, the source of all being,
eternal word and Spirit of life,
as it was in the beginning, is now and ever shall
be. Amen.

Or
Psalm 19, Psalm 96, Psalm 148 or the psalm of the
day from a lectionary; or any other psalm.

Glory to you, the source of all being,
eternal word and Spirit of life,
as it was in the beginning, is now and ever shall
be. Amen.

Pause.

Creator and Saviour,
we have exploited earth for our selfish ends,
turned our backs on the cycles of life
and forgotten we are your stewards.

Now soils become barren,
air and water become unclean,
species disappear
and humans are diminished.
In penitence we come to you.

Pause.

Creator, have mercy.
Redeemer, have mercy.
Sustainer, have mercy.

There may be silence, or a declaration of forgiveness.

Genesis 1:1–5, 20–31, Job 38:1–30, Isaiah 40:12–23,
Jeremiah 10:6–16 or the reading of the day from
a lectionary or reading scheme; or another Old
Testament reading.

For earth and sea and sky in the harmony
    of colour,
we give you thanks, O God.
For the air of the eternal seeping through
    the physical,
we give you thanks, O God.
For the everlasting glory dipping into time,
we give you thanks, O God.

For nature resplendent, growing beasts,
emergent crops, the energies of the city,
we give you thanks, O God.
For the person you sent to restore us when we fell
away from the goodness of your creation,
we give you thanks, O God.
For harmony restored through your Spirit moving
upon the turbulent waters of our lives,
we give you thanks, O God.
For the honour you give us of lives that flow in
the rhythm of your tides,
we give you thanks, O God.
For setting each of us, like the stars upon their
courses, within the orbit of your love,
we give you thanks, O God.

Matthew 6:25–34, Acts 14:8–18, Colossians 1:9–20,
Revelation 22:1–7 or the reading of the day from
a lectionary or reading scheme; or another New
Testament reading.

This may be followed by teaching, creative activity or
these words.

This we know, the earth does not belong to us;
the earth is God's and we will serve it.

This we know, we did not weave the web of life;
the earth is God's and we will serve it.
Whatever befalls the earth befalls the sons and
daughters of the earth;
the earth is God's and we will serve it.

The following prayers may be used.

Caring Father God, we offer to you
the fuels and forests,
the seas and soil,
the air and animals,
the textiles and technology of the world.
**May we take joy in your creation and steward it
for future generations.**

Worker Christ, we offer to you our workplace;
may we embody your presence in it.
Grace us to speak your peace and perfect order
into its atmosphere.
May we know your wisdom in all that will be
thought, decided and accomplished.
**Give us a fresh inspiration of truth and beauty
on which to draw as we work.**

Energising Spirit, we offer to you
our caring professions,
our emergency services,
our charities and voluntary helpers,
and all in need of your healing love.
**May this day be graced by our attentive
     presence,**
our careful listening and our loving service.

There may be open prayer.

In our dependence on the God of life,
may we cherish the precious earth;
the earth of the God of life,
the earth of the Christ of love,
the earth of the Holy Spirit.

God bless the sky that is above us,
the earth that is beneath us,
your image deep within us,
the day that lies before us.

Monday

midday prayer

Great Spirit, whose breath is felt in the
    soft breeze,
and whose life surges through socket and screen;
we seek your strength in the midst of the day.
May we, and the peoples of the world,
work in dignity and walk in the beauty of the day.
Blessed be God, the birther of life.
Blessed be God, the giver of light.
Blessed be God, the bestower of skills.

Psalm 67 is said as follows, or another psalm.

May God be merciful and bless us.
May his face smile with favour on us.
May your ways be known throughout the earth,
your saving power among people everywhere.

May the nations praise you, O God.
Yes, may all the nations praise you.

Let the whole world sing for joy,
**because you govern the nations with justice
and guide the people of the whole world.**

May the nations praise you, O God.
Yes, may all the nations praise you.

Then the earth will yield its harvests,
and God, our God, will richly bless us.
**Yes, God will bless us,
and people all over the world will fear him.**

Continue:

O Son of God, change our hearts.
Your Spirit composes the songs of the birds,
your creation is billions of wondrous miracles.
**Your creation is beautiful to look upon.
We ask of you just one more miracle:
beautify our souls.**
O God, you called all life into being;
your presence is around us now,
your Spirit enlivens all who work.
May your kingdom come on earth.
Impart to us wisdom to understand your ways,
to manage well the tasks of this day.

Make us co-creators with you
**that when day fades we may come to you
without shame.**

We pray for this world you have given us;
**for the planting of seeds
and for the nurturing of life
in the soils and commerce of the world.**

Sustain those who extract minerals, create
textiles, farm the land or develop technology.
**Encircle those who can neither sow nor reap
because human ills have drained them.**

Listen to the words of Christ:

Happy you who are gentle;
the earth belongs to you.
MATTHEW 5:5 (paraphrased)

You will labour,
but God will bless your work.
You will walk,
but God will bless your footsteps.
You will suffer,
but God will bless your tears.

Dwelling in the earth are the seeds of all.
Dwelling in the soul is the Son of God.

There may be singing or free prayer.

Bless all work done today
that enables the human family
to be clothed, fed and housed,
to travel and learn,
to communicate respectfully
and exchange wisely,
to craft and to celebrate
in everything reflecting your glory.
Good God, be with us in every experience of life.

There may be singing.

May you, our God, who dances with creation,
plants your likeness in all people
and works to restore all things,
send us out to fill the world with love. Amen.

Monday

evening prayer

We bless you, O God and forget not all
your benefits.
**We bless you for your creation, which is alive
with your glory.**
You nod and beckon to us through every stone
and star.
**As the sun sets in the west, may we settle down
with you.**

*There may be singing or else silent reflection on
God's creation.*

Either
Verses from Psalm 50 are said as follows.

The mighty God calls to the earth
from sun's rising to its sleep.
God the eternal source shines forth
perfect in glorious beauty.

**With fiery skies and raging storms
God calls to heaven, to earth:
'Bring to me those faithful souls
who give their hearts to me.'**

The mighty God requires our eyes
and beckons us to listen:
'You cannot earn a place near me,
for all that lives is mine:

**The cattle on a thousand hills,
the wildlife, trees and birds.
If I hungered, I'd not tell you
for all that lives is mine.**

So call to me in trial, in joy,
and give to me your thanks.
Worship by the way you live;
let gratitude abound.' [3]

Continue:

**Glory to you, the source of all being,
eternal word and Spirit of life,
as it was in the beginning, is now and ever
    shall be. Amen.**

Or
Psalm 29, Psalm 65, Psalm 136:1–9 or the psalm of
the day from a lectionary; or any other psalm.

Glory to you, the source of all being,
eternal word and Spirit of life,
as it was in the beginning, is now and ever shall
**   be. Amen.**

Genesis 2:4–9 and 18–25, Genesis 9:8–17, Isaiah 65:17–25,
Hosea 2:14–23 or the reading of the day from a lectionary
or reading scheme; or another Old Testament reading.

There may be silence.

Lord, you are my island,
in your bosom I nest.
You are the calm of the sea,
in that peace I rest.
You are the waves on the shore's
    glistening stones,
their sound is my hymn.
You are the song of the birds,
their tune I sing.
You are the sea breaking on rock,
I praise you with the swell.

You are the ocean that laps my being,
in you I dwell.

*Mark 4:26–32, Luke 8:22–25, Acts 17:16–31, Romans
8:18–30 or the reading of the day from a lectionary or
reading scheme; or another New Testament reading.*

There may be silence or teaching, or the following.

We bless you, Lord,
**for the beauty of the trees,
the softness of the air,
the fragrance of the grass.**

We bless you, Lord,
**for the soaring of the skies,
the rhythms of the earth,
the stillness of the night.**

We bless you, Lord,
**for the twinkling of the stars,
the freshness of the morning,
the dewdrops on the flower.**

We bless you, Lord,
for the taste of good food,

the trail of the sun,
and the life that never goes away.[4]

We give thanks for the moments of creation and
grace we have seen in this day.

Examples may be named.

Generosity of God, spilling over into creation,
we bless you for flowers and their wealth
of beauty,
for creatures and their glorious variety,
for seas and seasons and scents.
May we, too, reflect something of your
glorious generosity.

We pray for the well-being of the creation,
the healthfulness of the air,
the richness of the earth and its provisions
and the beauty of the whole world.
Creator, make us coworkers with you that the
earth and all who live upon it may reap a
full harvest.

Show us how to reflect your rhythms in our life
and work, and to conserve the world's
    rich resources.
**Help us to give all creatures their due respect,
    to tend cattle and crops with care.**

Guide science along wise and considerate ways
that we may fashion agriculture that
    truly enhances
and that we may sustain a vibrant environment.
May we too shine with the vibrancy of your love.

Peace to the land and all that grows on it.
Peace to the sea and all that swims in it.
Peace to the air and all that flies through it.
Peace with our God who calls us to serve.

Monday

night prayer

As the light fades and the work of the day is done,
as the flowers and the laptops close,
as the sun goes down and the world
    becomes still,
let us draw near to the Son of God.

**Lord God, King of the universe,
blessed be all creation,
for all life comes from you.
Blessed be the earth,
may it support our bed tonight.**

*There may be singing or playing of a creation-themed
song.*

Psalm 121 is said as follows.

I look up to the mountains –
does my help come from there?
My help comes from the Lord,
who made heaven and earth!

He will not let you stumble;
the one who watches over you will not slumber.
Indeed, he who watches over Israel
never slumbers or sleeps.

The Lord himself watches over you!
The Lord stands beside you as your
     protective shade.
The sun will not harm you by day,
nor the moon at night.

The Lord keeps you from all harm
and watches over your life.
The Lord keeps watch over you as you come
     and go,
both now and forever.

Continue:

We give you thanks that you are always present,
     in all things, each day and each night.

We give you thanks for your gifts of creation, life and friendship.
We give you thanks for the blessings of this day.

Blessings may be named in silence or aloud.

When we are calm and still, we can sense you,
   our Maker, we can feel your presence with us.
All that has been made stirs within us creation's
   song of praise.
We give you thanks for work completed. We give you thanks for rest at night.

Isaiah 40:28–31 is read:

Have you not known? Have you not heard? The Lord is the everlasting God, the Creator of the ends of the earth. He does not faint or grow weary; his understanding is unsearchable. He gives power to the faint and strengthens the powerless. Even youths will faint and be weary, and the young will fall exhausted; but those who wait for the Lord shall renew their strength, they shall mount up with wings like eagles, they shall run and not be weary, they shall walk and not faint.

Guardian of the planets, Kindler of the stars,
we pass into the darkness encompassed by you.

*There may be silence or singing, or a pause to reflect
upon the past day.*

**We offer you our concerns and the needs of
your creation.**

*There may be open prayer for the needs of creation and
current ecological issues.*

Thank you for your love for us, strong
and nurturing;
we give back our lives to you.
Thank you for our minds, bodies and souls;
we give back our lives to you.
Thank you for the past day;
we give back our lives to you.
After creating all things God rested;
we give back our lives to you.

Protect us through the hours of this night, be
they silent or stormy,
that we who are wearied by the changes and
chances of a restless world may rest upon
you eternally.

You created the world out of love; we return
   love to you.
Let us rest in God this night and awake in
   newness of life. Amen.

Tuesday

morning prayer

Glory to the Most High God, who has come to live
among us,
he has come to make peace in a hostile world.

Christ, born of the loveliest Mary,
you are with us in our birth.
Christ, brought up as a carpenter,
you are with us in our work.
Christ, friend of seeker and outcast,
you are with us in our friendships.
Christ, noble in suffering and death,
you are with us in our trials.
Christ, eternal Son of God,
you are with us evermore.

There may be singing.

Either
Psalm 8 is said as follows.

O Lord, our Lord, your majestic name fills
    the earth!
Your glory is higher than the heavens.
You have taught children and infants to tell of
    your strength,
silencing your enemies and all who oppose you.

When I look at the night sky and see the work of
    your fingers –
the moon and the stars you set in place –
what are mere mortals that you should think
    about them,
human beings that you should care for them?

Yet you made them only a little lower than God
and crowned them with glory and honour.
You gave them charge of everything you made,
putting all things under their authority –
the flocks and the herds and all the wild animals,
the birds in the sky, the fish in the sea,
and everything that swims the ocean currents.

O Lord, our Lord, your majestic name fills
    the earth!

Continue:

**Glory to God, Creator, Redeemer,
   Sustainer, forever.**

Or
*Psalm 20, Psalm 18:1–9, Psalm 45:1–7 or the psalm of
the day from a lectionary; or any other psalm.*

**Glory to God, Creator, Redeemer,
   Sustainer, forever.**

Dear Son of Mary, you took flesh to redeem us,
change our hearts.
Dear Son of God, you came to us with
   sacrificial love,
change our hearts.

There may be silence or these words of forgiveness.

The Son of God bounds towards us, reaching out
   a hand of reconciliation.
Let us take it, and listen to God's word.

*Isaiah 42:1–9, Hosea 11:1–9, Zephaniah 3:14–20, Joshua
5:13–15 or the reading of the day from a lectionary or
reading scheme; or another Old Testament reading.*

We bless you, our great God,
for you have set your people free.
You have raised up for us a mighty Saviour,
born of your servant David's family.
Through your holy prophets you promised of old
that you would save us from all who hate us.
You promised to show mercy to our forebears
and to remember your holy covenant.
You vowed to our ancestor Abraham
to set us free to worship you without fear.
The dawn from on high shall break upon us
**to shine on those in darkness and to guide us
into peace.**

*Philippians 2:5–11, Hebrews 4:14–5:10, Matthew
20:24–28, Romans 1:1–12 or the reading of the day
from a lectionary or reading scheme; or another New
Testament reading.*

There may be meditation or singing.

Babe of heaven, defenceless love,
you had to travel far from your home.
**Strengthen us on our pilgrimage of trust
on earth.**

King of glory, you accepted such humbling.
Clothe us with the garments of humility.

Child of Mary, your birth shows us the simplicity
of the Father's love.
Keep us in the simplicity of that love.

Child of glory, your coming shows us the wonder
of being human.
Help us to cherish every human life.

Christ who was heralded as Prince of Peace,
you came to remove the wall that divides one
people from another.
May walls of hostility come tumbling down,
especially…

Situations may be named.

Christ who comes with justice and peace,
we pray for the peace and well-being of the
whole world,
and of all the churches, especially…

Situations may be named.

The Lord's Prayer may be said or there may be singing.

May God help us to live simply, laugh often and
    love deeply.
May we see the face of Christ in everyone
    we meet.
**May everyone we meet see the face of Christ
    in us.**

Deep peace of the quiet earth to you,
deep peace of the still air to you,
deep peace of the forgiving heart to you,
deep peace of the Son of peace to you.

Tuesday

midday prayer

O Christ, you came among us to restore our
ancient beauty.
You became poor that we may become rich.

In the whirling wheels of the world,
you are with us.

When our day takes its toll,
you are with us.

In the clamour of voices,
you are with us.

When the sun shines on us,
you are with us.

When the world turns sour,
you are with us.

On suitable occasions anyone may add a sentence:

When…
You are with us.

There may be singing.

Make us aware, dear God,
of the eye that beholds us,
the hand that holds us,
the heart that loves us,
the presence that enfolds us.

Psalm 117 is said as follows, or another psalm.

Praise the Lord, all you nations.
Praise him, all you people of the earth.
For his unfailing love for us is powerful;
the Lord's faithfulness endures forever.
Praise the Lord!

The following may be said or sung:
Glory to you, O God of life,
Source of our being,
Eternal word and Holy Spirit.

These or other words of Christ are read:

> Happy are you who are peacemakers.
> You will be called God's children.
> MATTHEW 5:9 (paraphrased)

> My peace I give to you,
> not as the world gives do I give to you.
> JOHN 14:27 (paraphrased)

Silence, music or singing.

> Circle us, O God, for the rest of the day;
> keep harm without,
> keep good within.

Any may pray in the same pattern.

> Circle…

Name a person or situation.

> keep… without,
> keep… within.

Lead us from fear to trust.
Lead us from despair to hope.
Lead us from hate to love.
Lead us from war to peace.
Deep peace of the Son of peace
fill our hearts, our workplace, our world.

The final prayer may also be sung.

May the eternal glory shine upon us,
may the Son of Mary stay beside us,
may the life-giving Spirit be a canopy over us,
may the eternal three be ever with us.[5]

Tuesday
evening prayer

The peace of Christ has come into the world.
The peace of Christ has come into the world.

*Mary's Song may be said or sung twice to the tune
'Amazing Grace'.*

**Magnificat, magnificat,
praise God, my soul, praise God.
The proud are downed, the poor raised up,
Magnificat, my soul.**

Either
Verses from Psalm 132 are said as follows.

Lord, remember David,
and all the hardships he endured;
How he swore an oath to the Lord
and vowed a vow to the Mighty One of Jacob.

'I will not come under the roof of my house,
nor climb up into my bed;
I will not allow my eyes to sleep,
nor let my eyelids slumber;
until I find a place for the Lord,
a dwelling for the Mighty One of Jacob...'

Let us go to God's dwelling place;
let us fall upon our knees before his footstool.

Arise, O Lord, into your resting-place,
you and the ark of your strength.

Let your priests be clothed with righteousness;
let your faithful people sing with joy...

The Lord has sworn an oath to David;
in truth, he will not break it.

'A son, the fruit of your body, will I set upon
    your throne.
If your children keep my covenant and my
    testimonies that I shall teach them,
their children will sit upon your throne
    forevermore.'[6]

Continue:

**Glory to God, Creator, Redeemer,
     Sustainer, forever.**

Or
Psalm 21:1–7, Psalm 72:1–19, Psalm 89:1–4 and 19–29
or the psalm of the day from a lectionary; or any
other psalm.

**Glory to God, Creator, Redeemer,
     Sustainer, forever.**

We offer to you, Lord, the troubles of this day;
we lay down our burdens at your feet.

There may be a pause.

Forgive us our sins, give us your peace
and help us to receive your Word.
In the name of Christ. Amen.

Proverbs 8:1 and 22–31, Daniel 7:9–14, Genesis
18:1–15, Leviticus 26:1–13 or the reading of the day
from a lectionary or reading scheme; or another Old
Testament reading.

When the day takes its toll,
Christ bounds down the mountains towards us.
When we cry out in pain,
Christ bounds down the mountains towards us.
When all's well with the world,
Christ bounds down the mountains towards us.
When we need strength to do right,
Christ bounds down the mountains towards us.

Hebrews 1:1–4, John 19:1–7, Ephesians 2:12–22,
2 Corinthians 8:1–9 or the reading of the day from
a lectionary or reading scheme; or another New
Testament reading.

We give you thanks, our God, that you are always
    present, in all things, each day and each night.
We give you thanks for your gifts of creation, life
    and friendship.
We give you thanks for the particular blessings of
    this day.

There may be a brief pause, the naming of blessings,
singing in tongues or a sung response.

Christ, the peace of things above, and the peace
    of those below,
establish your peace in all creation and in your
    universal church.
Banish wars from the ends of the earth
and disperse those who delight in terror.

Child of glory, child of Mary, born in a stable,
King of all, you came to our wasteland; in our
    place suffered.
By choosing to be born as a child, you teach us to
    revere every human life.
May we never despise, degrade or destroy it.
Rather, help us sustain and preserve it.

Child of humanity, Trinity's only Son,
gentle and strong, from whose line we come,
bring your peace to your warring children.
Peace between rich and poor,
peace between races and religions,
peace between parents and children.

Bring your peace to those we name before
    you now.

There may be singing.

Help us, Lord, to guard our words,
to overcome hostility with love,
to make peace
in love of the King of life.

The final prayer may also be sung.

Deep peace of the running wave to you,
deep peace of the flowing air to you,
deep peace of the quiet earth to you,
deep peace of the shining stars to you,
deep peace of the Son of peace to you,
deep peace, deep peace.[7]

Tuesday

night prayer

Peace to us and to all who seek good.
**The peace of the Spirit be mine this night,
the peace of the Son be mine this night,
the peace of the Father be mine this night,
the peace of all peace be mine this night,
each morning and evening of my life.**

There may be singing or music may be played.

We offer to you, Lord, the troubles of this day;
we lay down our burdens at your feet.

There may be a pause.

Forgive us our sins, give us your peace
and help us to receive your word.
In the name of Christ. Amen.

Verses from Psalm 4 are read.

> Many people say, 'If only we might see some
>   good! Let some light from your face shine
>   upon us, O God!'
> You have put gladness in my heart more than
>   when all their material benefits abound.
> I will lie down and sleep in peace; for you alone,
>   O God, make me lie down in safety.[8]

Continue:

> May fears of the day recede, may treasures of
>   night draw near.
> **O Christ, Son of the living God,**
> **may your holy angels guard our sleep;**
> **may they hover around our beds**
> **and watch over us as we rest.**

> Let them reveal to us in our dreams visions of
>   your glorious truth.
> **May no fears or worries delay a prompt repose.**

The following or other words of Christ are read.

> Jesus said: 'Are you tired? Worn out?... Come to me. Get away with me and you'll recover your life. I'll show you how to take a real rest. Walk with me and work with me – watch how I do it. Learn the unforced rhythms of grace. I won't lay anything heavy or ill-fitting on you. Keep company with me and you'll learn to live freely and lightly.'
> MATTHEW 11:28–30 (MSG)

There may be meditation or sharing of thoughts.

> Gracious God, bless and keep our dear ones,
>   wherever they are, especially...

Names are spoken silently or aloud.

> **May heaven's peacekeepers encircle us all with
>   their outstretched arms;
> to protect us from the hostile powers,
> to put balm into our dreams,
> to give us contented, sweet repose.**

We lie down in peace knowing our sins
    are forgiven;
**we lie down in peace knowing death has
    no fear.**
We lie down in peace knowing strength in
    our weakness;
we lie down in peace knowing Jesus is near.

Peace to you.
We bless you now in the name of the Lord.
Peace to you.
**We bless you now in the name of the Prince
    of Peace.**
Peace to you.
Amen.

Wednesday

morning prayer

Come, Creator Spirit, fresh as the morning dew;
revive us and make us new.

Let us arise today in the Spirit's power.
In the place of fear,
God's strength to uphold me.
In the place of emptiness,
God's love to fill me.
In the place of confusion,
God's eye for my seeing,
God's wisdom to save me from false agendas
that harm both body and soul.

There may be singing.

Either
Psalm 32 is said as follows.

Oh what joy for those whose disobedience
is forgiven,
whose sin is put out of sight!

**Yes, what joy for those whose record the Lord
has cleared of guilt,
whose lives are lived in complete honesty!**

When I refused to confess my sin, my body
wasted away,
and I groaned all day long.

**Day and night your hand of discipline was
heavy on me.
My strength evaporated like water in the
summer heat.**

Finally, I confessed all my sins to you and
stopped trying to hide my guilt.
I said to myself, 'I will confess my rebellion to
the Lord.'
And you forgave me! All my guilt is gone.

**Therefore, let all the godly pray to you while
there is still time,
that they may not drown in the floodwaters
of judgement.**

For you are my hiding place; you protect me
   from trouble.
You surround me with songs of victory.

**The Lord says, 'I will guide you along the best
   pathway for your life.
I will advise you and watch over you.**

Do not be like a senseless horse or mule
that needs a bit and bridle to keep it
   under control.'

**Many sorrows come to the wicked,
but unfailing love surrounds those who trust
   the Lord.**

So rejoice in the Lord and be glad, all you who
   obey him!
Shout for joy, all you whose hearts are pure!

Continue:

**Glory to God, Creator, Redeemer,
   Sustainer, forever.**

Or
Psalm 63:1–8, Psalm 119:73–80, Psalm 147 or the psalm
of the day from a lectionary; or any other psalm.

Glory to God, Creator, Redeemer,
**   Sustainer, forever.**

From false desires and selfish deeds,
all-knowing One, deliver us.
From unworthy thoughts and prideful claims,
all-seeing One, deliver us.
From unclean hearts and petty ways,
all-cleansing One, deliver us.

Ezekiel 36:22–27, 1 Samuel 16:1–13, 2 Kings 2:1–15,
Haggai 2:1–8 or the reading of the day from a lectionary
or reading scheme; or another Old Testament reading.

Healer from heaven,
renew our bodies.
Healer from heaven,
revive our hearts.
Healer from heaven,
restore our souls.
God becomes one with us,
that we may be one with God.

Matthew 28:16–20, Acts 10:34–48, Ephesians 3:14–21,
1 Peter 4:12–19 or the reading of the day from a
lectionary or reading scheme; or another New
Testament reading.

There may be meditation and singing.

Come like fire and warm our hearts.
Come like wind and refresh our frames.
Come like water and revive our souls.
Come like the earth and nourish our being.

Holy Spirit, refine us,
that we may be just and true.
Sending Spirit, release us,
that we may touch lives for you.
Disturbing Spirit, recharge us,
that our jaded lives become new.

The following prayer may be sung or said.

On those whose day is drab,
come, Holy Spirit.
On those who harbour fear,
come, Holy Spirit.

On a parched land,
come, Holy Spirit.
On…
come, Holy Spirit.

There may be free prayer.

Eternal God and Father,
you create us by your power
and redeem us by your love:
guide and strengthen us by your Spirit,
that we may give ourselves in love and service
to one another and to you.[9]

There may be singing.

Lord, may your church grow in holiness and
    in number.
**Peace and blessing from the Spirit
and from the three who are ever one.**

May our hearts beat this day with the wings of
    the Wild Goose,
the untameable Spirit of God.

Wednesday

midday prayer

Holy Spirit,
come as a gentle breeze
that cools in the heat of the day,
come as the calming presence
that restores stillness to our being.
Wind of heaven,
blow away dross and deceits,
refresh our battered souls,
brace us for what is to come.

There may be silence or singing.

Psalm 23 may be said in the following way or a hymn
version may be sung.

God is my shepherd,
who refreshes me in green pastures,
restores me by quiet waters,

and leads me to the right ways.
With God I lack nothing I truly need.

Even though I walk through the valley
of the shadow of death
I will fear no evil, for you are with me,
your protecting staff comforts me.
With God I lack nothing I truly need.

You prepare a feast for me
even when hostile people surround me,
you anoint me with oil and my life overflows.
With God I lack nothing I truly need.

Surely goodness and mercy shall follow me
all the days of my life
and I will dwell in your presence forever.
With God I lack nothing I truly need.[10]

Continue:

Perfect comforter! Wonderful refreshment!
You make peace to dwell in our soul.
In our labour, you offer rest;
in temptation, strength.
From heaven shine forth with your glorious light.

Silence or singing.

When the day is dull,
may your Spirit open our eyes to hidden glories.
When we are tired and weary,
may your Spirit open our hearts to peace.
When the world is harsh and barren,
**may your Spirit open our lives to bring life
    and healing.**

One of the following is read.

The Spirit will show you what to say.
LUKE 12:12 (paraphrased)

The Holy Spirit joins with our spirit to affirm that
we are children of God.
ROMANS 8:16 (paraphrased)

The fruit of the Spirit is love, joy, peace,
patience, kindness, generosity, faithfulness,
gentleness, and self-control. There is no law
against such things.
GALATIANS 5:22–23 (paraphrased)

Alleluia.
Alleluia.

There may be singing, free prayer or the Lord's Prayer.

Holy Spirit, for the rest of the day renew in us,
joy in our work,
life in our being,
love in our relationships.

Wednesday

evening prayer

Kindling Spirit, come,
inflame our waiting hearts.
Consoling Spirit, come,
you know our every need.

There may be singing.

Either
Verses from Psalm 143 are said as follows.

Hear my prayer, O Lord; listen to my plea!
Answer me because you are faithful
    and righteous.
Don't put your servant on trial,
for no one is innocent before you…
I am losing all hope;
I am paralysed with fear.
I remember the days of old.

I ponder all your great works and think about
    what you have done.
I lift my hands to you in prayer.
I thirst for you as parched land thirsts for rain.
Come quickly, Lord, and answer me,
for my depression deepens.
Don't turn away from me, or I will die.
Let me hear of your unfailing love each morning,
    for I am trusting you.
Show me where to walk, for I give myself to you.
Rescue me from my enemies, Lord;
I run to you to hide me.
Teach me to do your will, for you are my God.
May your gracious Spirit lead me forward on a
    firm footing.
For the glory of your name, O Lord, preserve
my life.
Because of your faithfulness, bring me out of
this distress.

Continue:

Glory to God, Creator, Redeemer,
Sustainer, forever.

Or
Psalm 33:1–12, Psalm 81:1–10, Psalm 86:1–13 or the
psalm of the day from a lectionary; or any other psalm.

Glory to God, Creator, Redeemer,
Sustainer, forever.

There may be a pause.

Jeremiah 31:31–34, Ezekiel 11:14–25, Isaiah 44:1–8,
2 Chronicles 15:1–12 or the reading of the day from
a lectionary or reading scheme; or another Old
Testament reading.

The following may be said, or sung to the tune 'Veni
Creator Spiritus', or another suitable song may be sung.

Come, Holy Spirit, our souls inspire,
and lighten with eternal fire.
Implant in us your grace from above,
enter our minds and hearts with love.

O come, anointing Spirit of peace,
wellspring of life and gentleness.
Past ages called you the Paraclete;
with sevenfold gifts you make us complete.

You are the power of God's right hand,
promise of God to church and land.
Life-giving words to us impart;
illumine and transform our heart.

Into our souls your love now pour;
refresh our weak frame with strength
     and power.
Give grace and courage to endure;
cast far away our deadly foe.

Grant us your peace through every day,
with you as Guide upon the way
evil no more our souls shall harm,
we shall know as we are known.

Teach us the Trinity to know;
Father, Son and Spirit, too:
the three in one and one in three,
now and ever, eternally.

John 3:1–10, Romans 5:1–5, Galatians 3:1–5, Jude
17–25 or the reading of the day from a lectionary or
reading scheme; or another New Testament reading.

There may be meditation and singing.

Spirit of truth, look down upon a world in thrall
   to lies and illusions,
**work in the darkness to bring all things
   into light.**

Anointing Spirit, distribute among us your gifts:
**wisdom, understanding and strength,
knowledge, reverence and insight.**

*There may be silence, open prayer, the use of spiritual
gifts or singing.*

Great Creator of the glowing moon and
   shining stars,
Great Saviour of the miraculous birth and rising
   from death,
Great Spirit of the seers and sacred words;
**Work through our minds,
work through our dreams,
work through our mouths,
that we may become a sign of your presence.**

There may be free prayer.

Comforting Spirit, come to all who pass through
trial and to those we love, especially…

People and situations may be named.

There may be singing.

Send us out in the power of the Spirit,
to kindle many flames of love.

Wednesday

night prayer

We gather in the presence
of the God of wholeness,
in the presence of compassion's Son,
in the presence of the healing Spirit.
Tonight may we be one.

As we settle down this night,
we draw to mind the things of the day.

Time of silent recollection.

Psalm 103:1–5 is read.

Let all that I am praise the Lord;
with my whole heart, I will praise his holy name.
Let all that I am praise the Lord;
may I never forget the good things he does
for me.

He forgives all my sins
and heals all my diseases.
He redeems me from death
and crowns me with love and tender mercies.
He fills my life with good things.
My youth is renewed like the eagle's!

Continue:

Heal the places in us which have been hurt this
day, or in other days past.

Hebrews 13:5–6 is read.

Keep your lives free from the love of money, and
be content with what you have; for [God] has
said, 'I will never leave you or forsake you.' So we
can say with confidence, 'The Lord is my helper;
I will not be afraid. What can anyone do to me?'

Silence.

Spirit of the living God, present with us now,
we lay before you the activities of this day,
the activities of our minds, bodies and souls.

Time of silent recollection.

Become aware of your emotions and how they changed throughout this day.

Time of silent recollection.

Looking back, become aware of where God was present in this day, where you noticed the Divine presence at the time and where you did not, but do now.

Time of silent recollection.

Gracious one, forgive us for our negative emotions this day.
Forgive us.

Pause.

Forgive us for rush.
Forgive us.

Pause.

Forgive us for when we were not aware of your presence with us.
Forgive us.

Pause.

> Forgive us for lack of trust.
> **Forgive us.**

Pause.

> Forgive us for the ways we have marred your
>   image in us.
> **Forgive us.**

Pause.

> We open ourselves in love and faith to you,
>   O gracious three, Almighty one.
>
> Great Spirit, who broods over the sleeping world,
> as we sleep this night,
> restore the garment of our self-respect
> and remake us in your beauty.
> **Renew in us as we sleep,**
> **the stillness of our being,**
> **the soundness of our bodies,**
> **and bring to dawn our wholeness.**

Thursday

morning prayer

Birther of the human race,
you summon the day to dawn
and call us to live in communion.

**Thrice holy God, eternal three in one,
make your people holy, make your people one.
Stir up in us the flame
that burns out pride and power,
restore in us the trust
that brings the servant heart to flower.
Thrice holy God, come as the morning dew,
inflame in us your love
that draws all lesser loves to you.**

There may be singing.

Either
Psalm 113 is said as follows.

Hallelujah!
Give praise, you servants of the Lord;
praise the name of the Lord.
Let the name of the Lord be blessed,
from this time forth forevermore.
From the rising of the sun to its going down
let the name of the Lord be praised.
The Lord is high above all nations,
and his glory above the heavens.
Who is like the Lord our God,
who sits enthroned on high but stoops to behold
    the heavens and the earth?
He takes up the weak out of the dust
and lifts up the poor from the ashes.
He sets them with the princes,
with the princes of his people.
He makes the woman of a childless house
to be a joyful mother of children.[11]

Continue:

Glory to the Father, to the Son
and to the Spirit, one God who mothers us all.

Or
Psalm 46, Psalm 87, Psalm 112 or the psalm of the
day from a lectionary; or any other psalm.

**Glory to the Father, to the Son
and to the Spirit, one God who also mothers
us all.**

Holy Trinity, mutual sharing of self-giving love,
we confess to you that our lives
and our world are fragmented by sin.

There may be a pause.

Source of all,
have mercy on us.

Saviour of all,
have mercy on us.

Sustainer of all,
have mercy on us.

The merciful three reach out
to announce a loving reconciliation.
Thanks be to God.

*Genesis 12:1–9, Deuteronomy 10:12–22, Jeremiah
29:10–14, Ezekiel 18:5–9 or the reading of the day
from a lectionary or reading scheme; or another Old
Testament reading.*

May our sons be like plants that grow up strong.
Happy the people whose God is the
    Eternal Source.
May our daughters be like pillars crafted for a
    palace.
Happy the people whose God is the
    Eternal Source.
May our stores be filled with worthy goods.
Happy the people whose God is the
    Eternal Source.
May creatures and crops grow into well-being.
Happy the people whose God is the
    Eternal Source.
May our streets be free from clamour and crime.
Happy the people whose God is the
    Eternal Source.

From PSALM 144 (paraphrased)

*John 17:20–26, Galatians 3:23–29, Philippians
1:1–11, 1 John 3:11–17 or the reading of the day from
a lectionary or reading scheme; or another New
Testament reading.*

There may be meditation or singing.

Through word and sacrament you come to us,
   O Christ.
And we draw near to you.
God makes covenant with us.
And we offer God our lives.
The Trinity invites us into community.
With joy we share the divine life.

*After any of the following responses, examples of current
concerns may be offered to God.*

Ground of all being, all peoples come from you,
**may we honour one another and seek the
   common good.**

Reconciler of all people,
employers, employees and shareholders
are like fingers on your hand,
**may the wealth and work of the world
be available to all and for the exploitation
   of none.**

Unity of the world,
from you all peace, all justice flows,
**may we cherish the web of life and respect the
   rule of law.**

There may be singing.

> For my shield this day I call:
> a mighty power, the holy Trinity.
> **Faith in the three, trust in the one,**
> **creating all through love.**

The following blessing may be said or sung.

> **Into the sacred three I immerse you,**
> **into their power and peace I place you,**
> **may their breath be yours to live,**
> **may their love be yours to give.**
> **Into the sacred three I immerse you.**

Thursday

midday prayer

We gather in the name of God,
creating, redeeming, giving us life.

There may be singing.

God of justice, God of peace,
in the midst of the day
we take refuge in you.

Glory to you, Father,
glory to you.

Glory to you, Saviour,
glory to you.

Glory to you, Spirit,
glory to you.

Psalm 133 is read as follows:

> How good it is, how pleasing, for God's people to
>   live together in harmony.
> It is like precious ointment poured on the head.
>   It is like dew falling on the hills.
> This is where the Lord has promised his blessing,
>   life that never ends.[12]

Continue:

> We remember Jesus:
> gatherer of seekers; teller of stories;
> worker of wonders; breaker of bread;
> pourer of wine; giver of life.
> As Jesus washed his disciples' feet,
> **may we wash the feet of the world.**

> We weave this day
> **silence of knowing,**
> **clearness of seeing,**
> **grace of speaking.**

Pause.

We weave this day
humility of listening,
depth of understanding,
joy of serving.

Pause.

We weave this day
peace of being,
gift of loving,
power of meeting.

Pause.

One of the following New Testament readings is used.

'Where two or three are gathered in my name,
I am there.'
MATTHEW 18:20 (paraphrased)

'Do to others as you would have them do to you.'
MATTHEW 7:12 (paraphrased)

There may be meditation.

All may say or sing the following to the tune 'Bunessan'.

Christ be within me,
Christ be beside me,
Christ in the stranger,
Christ in the friend,
Christ in my speaking,
Christ in my thinking,
Christ in my working,
Christ at my end.

God of community,
Spirit of energy and change,
pour on us without reserve or distinction,
that we may have strength to plant your justice
     on earth.
Your kingdom come, your will be done,
on earth, as it is in heaven.
Your kingdom come.

Your kingdom come in the people or situations
     we now name.

People or situations may be named aloud or silently,
responding each time, 'Your kingdom come.'

The three who are over our head,
the three who provide our bread,
be with us wherever we tread.

Thursday

evening prayer

Holy, holy, holy is the eternal flame undying,
burning here among us in sacrificial love.

Candles may be lit.

We give you thanks, kindly light, that you led our
    forebears in the faith
through a cloud by day and a fire by night,
and that you ever lead your people on.
We give you thanks that you have led us to
    this place.
Pour forth your kindness on your people,
Creator, Saviour and radiant Spirit.

There may be singing.

Either
Psalm 82 is said as follows (NRSV).

God has taken his place in the divine council;
in the midst of the gods he holds judgement:
'How long will you judge unjustly and show
    partiality to the wicked?

Give justice to the weak and the orphan;
maintain the right of the lowly and
    the destitute.
Rescue the weak and the needy;
deliver them from the hand of the wicked.'

They have neither knowledge nor understanding,
they walk around in darkness;
all the foundations of the earth are shaken.
I say, 'You are gods,
children of the Most High, all of you;
nevertheless, you shall die like mortals,
and fall like any prince.'

Rise up, O God, judge the earth;
for all the nations belong to you!

Continue:

**Glory to the Birther, the Brother
and the Breather,
one God who mothers us all.**

Or
*Psalm 48, Psalm 99, Psalm 146 or the psalm of the
day from a lectionary; or any other psalm.*

**Glory to the Birther, the Brother
and the Breather,
one God who mothers us all.**

We offer to you, Lord, the troubles of this day;
we lay down our burdens at your feet.

There may be a pause.

Forgive us our sins, give us your peace,
and help us to receive your word.
In the name of Christ. Amen.

*Isaiah 2:1–4, Leviticus 19:9–18, Isaiah 56:1–8, Zephaniah
3:8–13 or the reading of the day from a lectionary or
reading scheme; or another Old Testament reading.*

Triune God, nurture the people through
   your church.

Through her pastors,
nourish us.

Through her teachers,
establish us.

Through her prophets,
envision us.

Through her musicians,
inspire us.

Through her saints,
sanctify us.

Through her givers,
bless us.

*Mark 3:31–35, Romans 12:9–21, Ephesians 4:1–16, James
3:13–18 or the reading of the day from a lectionary or
reading scheme; or another New Testament reading.*

There may be meditation and singing.

Lord Christ, you prayed for the unity of all
  who believe:
**may your churches rejoice in the communion
  of heaven and attain communion round one
  table on earth.**

Lord Christ, you call us to love our neighbours:
**may we and our local communities seek the
  common good.**

Lord Christ, through bread and wine you give
  us signs of your presence transforming
  all creation:
**may we and those in the media glimpse this
  vision and reflect it to the world.**

We pray for reconciliation to be experienced
  and memories healed in all parts of the
  universal church.

Silent prayer.

There may also be free prayer or the following.

O God, grant us unity.
Bless the oppressed with justice and the
    oppressor with repentance.
Draw all people home to you.

Pause.

Deliver the downtrodden, pity the unnoticed.
Raise the fallen, show yourself to the needy.

Pause.

Heal the sick, bring back those who have strayed.

Pause.

Feed the hungry, lift up the weak.
Remove the prisoners' chains.

Pause.

May every people come to know
that you are God, that Christ is your child,
that we are your people.

There may be singing.

Jesus Christ, light of the world, by your cross
you have overcome all darkness that oppresses.
**Come and shine on us in our communities,
that we may grow and live together in
   your love,
which makes us one with all humanity.**

**The grace of our Lord Jesus Christ,
the love of God
and the fellowship of the Holy Spirit
be with us all evermore. Amen.**

Thursday

night prayer

Three candles may be lit as the following words are said by one or three people.

I light a light in the name of the Father who embraces us.

I light a light in the name of the Son who enfolds us.

I light a light in the name of the Spirit who encircles us.

**Our God is one,
the God from whom all people come,
one earth is the bed on which we make
our home,
one is the air that all creatures breathe.**

Psalm 111 is said as follows.

> Mighty One,
> I give you thanks with my whole heart.
> Great are your works:
> all who sense their wonder study them.
> Your work overflows with majesty and honour
> and your righteousness lasts forever.
> You are gracious and full of mercy.
> You provide food for those who honour you.
> You are faithful and just in all you do.
> Reverence for you is the beginning of wisdom;
> all those who practise it have good
>   understanding.[13]

There may be singing or music.

> We thank you for your presence through the
>   day and for friends who have helped us on
>   our way.
> **As shadows fall and the wheels of the world
>   grow still, forgive us for our failures in love.**

> Visit the place in which we rest this night and
>   drive away all that would harm.
> **May holy angels preserve us in peace.**

Support us, Lord,
through life's troubles each day,
until the shadows lengthen and evening comes,
the fever of life is over and our work is done.
**Then, Lord, in your mercy, give us a holy rest
    and peace at the last.**

There may be silence.

1 Peter 3:8–12 is read.

Finally, all of you, have unity of spirit, sympathy,
love for one another, a tender heart, and a hum-
ble mind. Do not repay evil for evil or abuse for
abuse, but, on the contrary, repay with a blessing. It is for this that you were called – that you
might inherit a blessing. For 'those who desire
to love life and to see good days, let them keep
their tongues from evil and their lips from speaking deceit; let them turn away from evil and do
good; let them seek peace and pursue it. For
the eyes of the Lord are on the righteous, and
his ears are open to their prayer. But the face of
the Lord is against those who do evil.'

Either of the following sets of prayers may be used.

On your world, Lord,
your love descend this night.
On your church, Lord,
your love descend this night.
On all who work, Lord,
your love descend this night.
Where there is strife, Lord,
your love descend this night.
Where there is neglect, Lord,
your love descend this night.
On all who sleep, Lord,
your love descend this night.

Other prayers may be added in the same way.

On…
your love descend this night.

Or

Circle the world, Lord,
keep grudges without, keep friendship within.
Circle the world, Lord,
keep bickering without, keep trust within.
Circle those we bring before you now.

People may be named aloud or in silence.

There may be singing.

Kindle in our hearts, O God, the flame of that love
which never ceases, that it may burn in us this
night till we shine forever in your presence.
**God with us lying down, God with us rising up.
Christ with us sleeping, Christ with us
waking. Spirit with us now, Spirit with us
evermore. Amen.**

Friday

morning prayer

On this day of Christ's suffering and death,
let us be one with him in his wounds.
We seek to tread in the steps of Christ,
in the steps of Christ, our champion and King,
who has shown us the way,
when strong, when weak.

Either
Verses from Psalm 69 are said as follows.

Save me, O God,
for the floodwaters are up to my neck.

Deeper and deeper I sink into the mire;
I can't find a foothold.
I am in deep water,
and the floods overwhelm me.

I am exhausted from crying for help;
my throat is parched.
My eyes are swollen with weeping,
waiting for my God to help me…

Don't let those who trust in you be ashamed
   because of me,
O Sovereign Lord of Heaven's Armies.
Don't let me cause them to be humiliated,
O God of Israel.

For I endure insults for your sake;
humiliation is written all over my face.

Even my own brothers pretend they don't
   know me;
they treat me like a stranger…

Answer my prayers, O Lord,
for your unfailing love is wonderful.
Take care of me,
for your mercy is so plentiful.

Don't hide from your servant;
answer me quickly, for I am in deep trouble!
Come and redeem me;
free me from my enemies.

Continue:

Glory to the Maker, glory to the Son,
glory to the Spirit, ever three and ever one.

Or
Psalm 40, Psalm 56, Psalm 70 or the psalm of the day
from a lectionary; or any other psalm.

Glory to the Maker, glory to the Son,
glory to the Spirit, ever three and ever one.

Jesus, you were driven to the sands
by the searching Spirit,
strip from us what is not of you.

Confession is made in silence, or as follows.

Forgive us;
for our selfish deeds,
our empty speech
and the words with which we have wounded.

Pause.

Forgive us;
**for our false desires,
our vengeful attitudes
and for what we have left untended.**

Pause.

Holy Jesus, hanged on a tree, victorious
    over death;
**forgive us for these sins,
free us from these evils
and power us into new ways.**

There may be singing.

*Genesis 22:1–14, Isaiah 53:1–12, Hosea 14:1–7, Micah
7:18–20 or the reading of the day from a lectionary or
reading scheme; or another Old Testament reading.*

Jesus, Saviour of the world,
come to us in your mercy.
We look to you to save and help us.

By your cross and life laid down,
you set your people free.
We look to you to save and help us.

When your disciples were about to perish
you reached down and saved them.
We look to you to come to our help.

In the greatness of your mercy,
free us from our chains.
Forgive the sins of all your people.

Come now and dwell with us, Lord Christ Jesus.
Hear our prayer and be with us always.

And when you come in your glory,
**make us to be one with you and to share the life
of your kingdom.**

*Mark 10:35–45, 1 Corinthians 1:18–25, Colossians
2:6–15, 1 John 1:5—2:2 or the reading of the day from
a lectionary or reading scheme; or another New
Testament reading.*

There may be silence.

Jesus, broken on the cross,
we bring to you those suffering from
broken dreams, broken relationships and
broken promises.

Pause or give names.

Lord Jesus Christ,
have mercy on them.

Jesus, who lost everything,
we bring to you those who have suffered loss
of work, mobility and well-being.

Pause or give names.

Lord Jesus Christ,
have mercy on them.

Jesus, defenceless victim,
we bring to you those who are victims of
    violence, abuse and false accusation.

Pause or give names.

Lord Jesus Christ,
have mercy on them.

Jesus, alone and destitute,
we bring to you those who are lonely,
homeless and hungry.

Pause or give names.

Lord Jesus Christ,
have mercy on them.

Saviour, you died that we may be brought back
    to you.
Turn the hearts of those who do not yet
    know you.

Pause or give names.

Lord Jesus Christ,
have mercy on them.

The Lord's Prayer may be said.

There may be singing.

**May the Christ who walks with wounded feet
walk with us on the road.
May the Christ who serves with wounded hands
stretch out our hands to serve.
May the Christ who loves with wounded heart
open our hearts to love.**

Friday

midday prayer

Jesus, master carpenter of Nazareth,
who, through wood and nails,
won our full salvation,
wield well your tools in this,
your workshop,
that we who come to you rough-hewn
may here be fashioned into a truer beauty
by your hand.[14]

Psalm 31:1–5 is read as follows.

O Lord, I have come to you for protection;
don't let me be disgraced.
Save me, for you do what is right.

Turn your ear to listen to me;
rescue me quickly.
Be my rock of protection,
a fortress where I will be safe.

You are my rock and my fortress.
For the honour of your name, lead me out of
    this danger.
Pull me from the trap my enemies set for me,
for I find protection in you alone.

I entrust my spirit into your hand.
Rescue me, Lord, for you are a faithful God.

There may be silence or singing.

We draw aside in the midst of the day.
Where there is poverty and hunger,
where children are harmed and mistreated,
where people are maimed and broken,
we plead for your justice.

Where there is cruelty and hatred,
where there is greed and suspicion,
where there is homelessness and war,
we plead for your justice.

Lord Jesus, at this hour you hung on the cross,
stretching out your arms in love to all.
May the peoples of the world
be drawn to your uplifted love,

**especially those with whom we shall work
this day.**

Give us the will to share our bread with
the hungry,
to give room to those who feel rejected
and to reach out to those in need.
**We pray for those whose tasks are
backbreaking, whose bodies are enslaved
or whose spirits are crushed.**

*There may be silence in which we hold before the cross
those for whom we pray.*

These words of Jesus are said.

Happy you who hunger for justice;
you will be filled.
Happy you who show mercy;
you will receive mercy.
Happy you who weep;
you will laugh.
MATTHEW 5:6–7, 4 (paraphrased)

There may be singing.

Lord Jesus, in the midst of malice and mockery
you found peace to remain in your Father's will.
When we are mocked or maligned,
give us peace to remain in our Father's will.

The Lord's Prayer is said in the traditional form or as
follows.

Our Father in heaven,
honoured be your name,
your kingdom come,
your will be done
on earth, as in heaven.
Give us this day our daily supplies
and forgive us our sins,
as we forgive those who sin against us.
Lead us not into time of trial,
but deliver us from evil.
For yours is the kingdom, the power and
    the glory,
forever and ever. Amen.

Friday

evening prayer

Sacrificial love lingers still among us,
calling us to wait and to watch.

Eternal Light,
shine into our hearts.

Eternal Goodness,
deliver us from evil.

Eternal Power,
strengthen us.

Eternal Wisdom,
scatter the darkness of our ignorance.

Eternal Pity,
have mercy on us.

**With our whole being we shall seek your face
until we are brought to your holy presence.**

There may be a meditative chant or singing.

Either
Psalm 103:1–18 is said as follows.

Let all that I am praise the Lord;
with my whole heart, I will praise his holy name.

**Let all that I am praise the Lord;
may I never forget the good things he does
  for me.**

He forgives all my sins
and heals all my diseases.

**He redeems me from death
and crowns me with love and tender mercies.**

He fills my life with good things.
My youth is renewed like the eagle's!

**The Lord gives righteousness
and justice to all who are treated unfairly.**

He revealed his character to Moses
and his deeds to the people of Israel.

The Lord is compassionate and merciful,
slow to get angry and filled with unfailing love.

He will not constantly accuse us,
nor remain angry forever.

He does not punish us for all our sins;
he does not deal harshly with us, as we deserve.

For his unfailing love toward those who fear him
is as great as the height of the heavens above
   the earth.

He has removed our sins as far from us
as the east is from the west.

The Lord is like a father to his children,
tender and compassionate to those who
   fear him.

For he knows how weak we are;
he remembers we are only dust.

Our days on earth are like grass;
like wildflowers, we bloom and die.

**The wind blows, and we are gone –
as though we had never been here.**

But the love of the Lord remains forever
with those who fear him.

**His salvation extends to the children's children
of those who are faithful to his covenant,
of those who obey his commandments!**

Or
*Psalm 42, Psalm 77, Psalm 130 or the psalm of the
day from a lectionary; or any other psalm.*

There may be silence.

*Numbers 21:4–9, Isaiah 1:10–20, Isaiah 44:21–23,
Zechariah 12:10–13:1 or the reading of the day from
a lectionary or reading scheme; or another Old
Testament reading.*

Lord, you were tested by the evil one;
break in us the hold of power and pride.

You knew deep tears and weaknesses;
help us to be vulnerable for you.

You followed to the end the way of the cross;
**help us to be faithful to you to the end of
    our days.**

A Kyrie ('Lord, have mercy') may be sung.

*Luke 23:32–43, 2 Corinthians 5:11–21, Hebrews
2:10–18, Revelation 5:1–14 or the reading of the day
from a lectionary or reading scheme; or another Old
Testament reading.*

There may be meditation or singing.

Lord Jesus, you died to save us,
not from suffering, but from ourselves;
not from injustice, but from being unjust.
You died that we might live as you did,
who died to yourself.
**In union with witnesses and martyrs of Christ;
in communion with all who have died
in the faith of Christ,
we commit ourselves to our living God.**

As we seek to be faithful to you and struggle to
　　establish justice,
we bring to you those who are in chains.

Pause or free prayer.

We bring to you people who are persecuted
　　or oppressed,
the homeless, the hungry and those in
　　grinding poverty.

Pause or free prayer.

We bring to you those who are abused, belittled
　　or marginalised.

Pause or free prayer.

We bring to you those who are in pain behind
　　closed doors.

Pause or free prayer.

We bring to you those who are locked
　　into hatred.

Pause or free prayer.

> We bring to you all the world for which you died.
> **Christ, victorious over evil, fill their hearts and
>   ours with generous love.**

There may be singing.

> We go in the sign of the cross of Christ.

Make the sign of the cross.

> **The cross above us to lead us through,
> the cross before us to keep us true,
> the cross behind us to shield us from ill,
> this day and always. Amen.**

Friday

night prayer

Shadows darken this day;
the day Christ was laid in a grave.
The darkness shall not engulf us;
for with you the darkness is light.
Lord, by your cross and precious death;
save us from the powers of evil,
save us from another's harm,
save us from our selfish failings,
come this night and give us calm.

There may be singing.

Psalm 90:1–12 is read as follows, or verses from another psalm.

Lord, through all the generations
you have been our home!
Before the mountains were born,

before you gave birth to the earth and the world,
from beginning to end, you are God.

You turn people back to dust, saying,
'Return to dust, you mortals!'
For you, a thousand years are as a passing day,
as brief as a few night hours.
You sweep people away like dreams
**   that disappear.**
They are like grass that springs up in
**   the morning.**
In the morning it blooms and flourishes,
but by evening it is dry and withered.

We wither beneath your anger;
we are overwhelmed by your fury.
You spread out our sins before you –
our secret sins – and you see them all.
We live our lives beneath your wrath,
ending our years with a groan.

Seventy years are given to us!
Some even live to eighty.
But even the best years are filled with pain
**   and trouble;**
soon they disappear, and we fly away.

Who can comprehend the power of your anger?
Your wrath is as awesome as the fear
   you deserve.

**Teach us to realise the brevity of life,
so that we may grow in wisdom.**

There may be silence.

Created, evolved, accepted, loved: in response to
   this grace of God let us confess our sins, that
   when our bodies become but ashes we may
   live with you forever.

Let us reflect on the things that distance us
   from Christ.

Pause.

1 John 1:8–9 is read as follows (NLT).

If we claim we have no sin, we are only fooling
ourselves and not living in the truth. But if we
confess our sins to him, he is faithful and just
to forgive us our sins and to cleanse us from all
wickedness.

Lord God, forgive us our sins.
Lord, forgive.

'Kyrie Eleison' or similar may be sung or played.

As he was dying a martyr's death Jesus said:
'My God, my God, why have you forsaken me?'

Christ forsaken,
have mercy on all who are forsaken.
Christ afraid,
have mercy on all who are afraid.
Christ betrayed,
have mercy on all who are betrayed.

People may mention, in silence or aloud, those who need our prayers.

Great God who mothers us all, gather the
sufferings of all into the communion of the
crucified Christ.
**Shield and deliver them and look on them with
your merciful gaze.**

There may be singing.

Jesus said: 'Father into your hands I entrust
my spirit';
Father, into your hands we entrust our spirits.
Father, as we sit at the foot of the cross,
Father, into your hands we entrust our spirits.

Either
*Simeon's song may be sung as the hymn 'Faithful
vigil ended' or it may be said as follows.*

Lord, you now have set your servant free
to go in peace as you have promised.

For these eyes of mine have seen the Saviour
whom you have prepared
for all the world to see;

A light to reveal you to the nations
and the glory of your people.

O Christ who at this evening hour
rested in the tomb
and made it become a bed of hope,
visit this place tonight,
that we may pass through the death of sleep
and rise from our beds in hope of life eternal.

Lord, give us a peaceful night and prepare us
for a good ending to life.

I make the sign of the cross of Christ.

Make the sign of the cross.

My Christ, my shield, my Saviour;
each day, each night, in light, in dark,
my treasure, my dear one, my eternal home.
Amen.

Saturday

morning prayer

Life-giving God, the world lies open before you
and you summon the day to dawn.

Open our being
and we shall show life.

Open our hearts
and we shall show love.

Open our mouths
and we shall show praise.

There may be singing.

Either
Psalm 97 is said as follows.

The Lord is king! Let the earth rejoice!
Let the farthest coastlands be glad.

Dark clouds surround him.
Righteousness and justice are the foundation
    of his throne.

Fire spreads ahead of him
and burns up all his foes.
His lightning flashes out across the world.
The earth sees and trembles.

The mountains melt like wax before the Lord,
before the Lord of all the earth.
The heavens proclaim his righteousness;
every nation sees his glory.

Those who worship idols are disgraced –
all who brag about their worthless gods –
for every god must bow to him.

Jerusalem has heard and rejoiced,
and all the towns of Judah are glad
because of your justice, O Lord!
For you, O Lord, are supreme over all the earth;
you are exalted far above all gods.

You who love the Lord, hate evil!
He protects the lives of his godly people
and rescues them from the power of the wicked.

Light shines on the godly,
and joy on those whose hearts are right.
May all who are godly rejoice in the Lord
and praise his holy name!

Continue:

Glory to the Father, glory to the Son,
glory to the Spirit, ever three and ever one.

Or
Psalm 5, Psalm 66, Psalm 145 or the psalm of the day
from a lectionary; or any other psalm.

Glory to the Father, glory to the Son,
glory to the Spirit, ever three and ever one.

All that moves on the earth,
bless your God.

All that swims in the water,
bless your God.

All that flies in the air,
give glory to God who nurtures us all.

Parents and children,
bless your God.

Friends and lovers,
bless your God.

Musicians and sports people,
give glory to God who nurtures us all.

Parks and play areas,
bless your God.

Streets and shops,
bless your God.

Homes and gardens,
give glory to God who nurtures us all.

In all we do, let our lives today
give glory to God who nurtures us all.

1 Chronicles 17:1–14, Ecclesiastes 3:1–15, Proverbs 3:1–12, Isaiah 52:7–10 or the reading of the day from a lectionary or reading scheme; or another Old Testament reading.

We believe, O God of all gods,
that you are the eternal God of life.

We believe, O God of all peoples,
that you are the eternal God of love.

We believe that you create earth and seas and
 skies;
**we believe that you create us in your image and
 give us eternal worth.**

We honour you with our whole being
and consecrate this day to you.

*Mark 4:1–20, Luke 10:1–11, Romans 14:7–19, 2 Peter
1:1–11 or the reading of the day from a lectionary or
reading scheme; or another New Testament reading.*

There may be meditation and singing.

All-creative one,
 thank you for gifts of engineering and design,
  provision and organisation,
 which maintain the fabric of our lives.

*Examples of people or things are brought to mind aloud
or in silence.*

Make whole the leisure and activity of this day;
fill its moments with glimpses of your glory.

Our Father in heaven,
hallowed be your name,
your kingdom come
your will be done
on earth, as in heaven.

In our pleasures,
your kingdom come.

In our leaders,
your kingdom come.

In our gatherings,
your kingdom come.

On the roads,
your kingdom come.

Online,
your kingdom come.

Other activities may be named using this structure.

In…
your kingdom come.

In each thing we do this day,
your kingdom come.

Give us this day our daily supplies
and forgive us our sins,
as we forgive those who sin against us.
Lead us not into temptation,
but deliver us from evil.
For the kingdom, the power
and the glory are yours,
now and forever. Amen.

There may be singing.

May we do this day on earth
as the saints do in heaven.
May we live this day in your light
and walk in the hope of your kingdom.

Saturday

midday prayer

God of life!
God of peace!
God of time!
Be with us in the middle of the day.

Pause.

God of truth!
God of love!
God of wisdom!
Be with us in the middle of the day.

Pause.

God of work!
God of play!
God of rest!
Be with us in the middle of the day.

There may be singing.

Psalm 119:9–16 or another section of the psalm is read.

How can a young person stay pure?
By obeying your word.
I have tried hard to find you –
don't let me wander from your commands.

I have hidden your word in my heart,
that I might not sin against you.
I praise you, O Lord;
teach me your decrees.

I have recited aloud
all the instructions you have given us.
I have rejoiced in your laws
as much as in riches.

I will study your commandments
and reflect on your ways.
I will delight in your decrees
and not forget your word.

Continue:

Christ, who multiplied bread,
bring fullness to our day.
Christ, who turned water into wine,
bring richness to our day.
Christ, who stilled the storm,
bring peace to our day.

Happy you who are poor;
yours is the kingdom of God.
Happy you who are pure in heart;
you will see God.
MATTHEW 5:3, 8 (paraphrased)

There may be silence and singing.

Christ of the crowds,
Be in our busyness.
Christ of the open spaces,
Be in our quietness.
Christ of the eating places,
Be in our enjoyment.
Christ of the unplanned meeting,
Be in our conversations.

There may be silent or free prayer.

May the saints and the Saviour watch over us
and keep us true in all we do.
**May we live the rest of this day
in the joy of the Saviour's will.**

Saturday

evening prayer

Let us go for a while to the courts of heaven
and join with the saints in praise.

Either
Verses from Psalm 139 are said as follows.

O Lord, you have examined my heart
and know everything about me.
You know when I sit down or stand up.
You know my thoughts even when I'm far away.

**You see me when I travel
and when I rest at home.
You know everything I do.
You know what I am going to say
even before I say it, Lord.**

You go before me and follow me.
You place your hand of blessing on my head.

Such knowledge is too wonderful for me,
too great for me to understand!

I can never escape from your Spirit!
I can never get away from your presence!
If I go up to heaven, you are there;
if I go down to the grave, you are there.

If I ride the wings of the morning,
if I dwell by the farthest oceans,
even there your hand will guide me,
and your strength will support me.

I could ask the darkness to hide me
and the light around me to become night –
but even in darkness I cannot hide from you.
To you the night shines as bright as day.
Darkness and light are the same to you.

You made all the delicate, inner parts of my body
and knit me together in my mother's womb.
Thank you for making me so wonderfully
    complex!
Your workmanship is marvellous – how well
    I know it…

How precious are your thoughts about me,
O God.
They cannot be numbered!
I can't even count them;
they outnumber the grains of sand!
And when I wake up, you are still with me.

Continue:

Glory to God, Source of our being,
Eternal Word, and Holy Spirit,
one God who mothers us all.

Or
Psalm 25:1–10, Psalm 91, Psalm 125 or the psalm of
the day from a lectionary; or any other psalm.

Glory to God, Source of our being,
eternal word and Holy Spirit,
one God who mothers us all.

There may be singing.

Isaiah 32:1–8, Jeremiah 23:1–8, Amos 9:11–15, Zechariah
8:1–8, 20–23 or the reading of the day from a lectionary
or reading scheme; or another Old Testament reading.

If our mouths were as full of song as the sea,
our tongues with joyful sounds
like the roar of its waves,
our lips with praise like the outspread sky,

we still could not thank you enough
for the good you have done to us
and our forebears.

If our eyes were shining like the sun and
    the moon,
our hands stretched out like eagles' wings in
    the air,
our feet as swift as the wild deer,

we still could not thank you enough, Yahweh,
for the good you have done to us
and our forebears.

You rescued us from the tyrant,
you freed us from slavery.

In times of famine you fed us,
in times of plenty you built us up.

From violence you delivered us,
from plagues you saved us.

**Therefore to you who breathed life into us
we shall give praise with all our breath,
honour with all our memory,
worship with all our being.**[15]

*Matthew 25:31–46, Colossians 3:1–4, Hebrews
12:18–28, Revelation 1:1–8 or the reading of the day
from a lectionary or reading scheme; or another New
Testament reading.*

There may be meditation or singing.

God of the call, as we give thanks for the saints,
we pray for those who feel thwarted in
    their vocation;
**may they do on earth as the saints do
   in heaven.**

God from whom all truth and justice flow,
we pray for the rule of law to prevail;
may we do on earth as the saints do in heaven.

God of resurrection, in their worship
may our churches bring honour to you,
joy to the people and healing to the land;
**may they do on earth as the saints do
   in heaven.**

There may be open prayer and singing.

Let us bless the Lord.
**Yours, O Lord, are the greatness, the power,
the glory, the victory and the majesty,
forever and ever. Amen.**

Saturday

night prayer

On occasions when Saturday night prayer is extended as a night vigil, the reading for Sunday's main worship may be read and pondered, or there may be the slow, thoughtful repetition of the Jesus Prayer, 'Lord Jesus Christ, Son of God, have mercy.'

Eternal Creator of the weeks and years, as this
    week draws to a close,
draw close to us as we draw close to you.
Eternal Creator of the days and nights, as
    darkness deepens,
draw near to us as we draw near to you.

Most merciful God, we confess to you before the
    company of heaven and one another that we
    have sinned in thought, word and deed, and in
    what we have failed to do.

Forgive us our sins, heal us by your Spirit and raise us to new life in Jesus Christ.

Psalm 119:52–62 or another section of the psalm is read.

I meditate on your age-old regulations;
O Lord, they comfort me.
I become furious with the wicked,
because they reject your instructions.

Your decrees have been the theme of my songs
wherever I have lived.
I reflect at night on who you are, O Lord;
therefore, I obey your instructions.

This is how I spend my life:
obeying your commandments.

Lord, you are mine!
I promise to obey your words!
With all my heart I want your blessings.
Be merciful as you promised.

I pondered the direction of my life,
and I turned to follow your laws.
I will hurry, without delay,
to obey your commands.

Evil people try to drag me into sin,
but I am firmly anchored to your instructions.
I rise at midnight to thank you
for your just regulations.

*The following may be sung to the traditional tune,
or said:*

Before the ending of the day,
Creator of the world, we pray,
that you, with steadfast love, would keep
your watch around us while we sleep.

From evil dreams defend our sight,
from fears and terror of the night;
tread under foot our deadly foe,
that we no sinful thought may know.

O Father, what we ask be done,
through Jesus Christ, your only Son
and Holy Spirit, by whose breath,
our souls are raised to life from death.
Amen.

Hebrews 3:12—4:1 or another passage is read.

Take care, brothers and sisters, that none of you may have an evil, unbelieving heart that turns away from the living God. But exhort one another every day, as long as it is called 'today', so that none of you may be hardened by the deceitfulness of sin. For we have become partners of Christ, if only we hold our first confidence firm to the end. As it is said, 'Today, if you hear his voice, do not harden your hearts as in the rebellion.' Now who were they who heard and yet were rebellious? Was it not all those who left Egypt under the leadership of Moses? And with whom was he angry for forty years? Was it not those who sinned, whose bodies fell in the wilderness? And to whom did he swear that they would not enter his rest, if not to those who were disobedient? So we see that they were unable to enter because of unbelief. Therefore, while the promise of entering his rest is still open, let us take care that none of you should seem to have failed to reach it.

There may be silence.

In our tiredness
be our rest,
in our stumbling
be our shield.
Into our place of darkness, into our place of strife,
    into our fears and worries,
come with eternal life.

Let us bring before God the concerns of this day.

These may be mentioned aloud or in silence.

There may be singing or silence.

When we neglect you,
remind us of your presence;
when we are frightened,
give us courage;
when we are tempted,
give us the power to resist;
when we are anxious and worried,
give us peace;
when we are weary in service,
renew our tired frame.

Jesus,
leader of apostles,
teacher of evangelists,
strength of martyrs,
friend of the poor,
crown of saints,
lead us through the night into a day of renewal.
**May we rest secure in your love and rise up to
serve you with joy. Come with the breaking
of the day and meet us in the breaking of
bread. Amen.**

Notes

1   Prayer attributed to St Brigid.
2   Psalm 104 has been paraphrased.
3   Psalm 50 has been paraphrased.
4   Inspired by words of Chief Dan George (1889–1981), Tsleil-Waututh Nation, Canada.
5   Ray Simpson, *Celtic Hymn Book* (Kevin Mayhew Ltd, 2005), no. 132. Used with kind permission.
6   The Episcopal Church, *The Book of Common Prayer* (Church Publishing Inc, 1979). This publication is in the public domain.
7   Ray Simpson, *Celtic Hymn Book* (Kevin Mayhew Ltd, 2005), no. 40. Used with kind permission.
8   Psalm 4:6–8 has been paraphrased.
9   The Church of England, *The Alternative Service Book* (Central Board of Finance of the Church of England, 1980).
10 Psalm 23 has been paraphrased.
11 The Episcopal Church, *The Book of Common Prayer*.
12 Psalm 133 has been paraphrased.
13 Psalm 111 has been paraphrased.
14 Arthur Gray Butler (1831–1909).
15 Traditional Jewish sabbath prayer. See **en.wikipedia.org/wiki/Nishmat**.

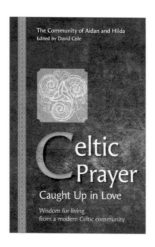

With contributions from 30 members of the dispersed Community of Aidan and Hilda, *Celtic Prayer: Caught Up in Love* explores 20 different ways of praying from the Celtic Christian tradition. Accessible and inspiring, it will refresh your spirit and draw you deeper into knowing God.

Celtic Prayer: Caught Up in Love
Wisdom for living from a modern Celtic community
Edited by David Cole

978 1 80039 053 9 £12.99

brfonline.org.uk

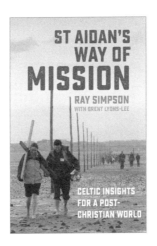

Surveying the life and times of Aidan of Lindisfarne, this book draws insights into missional approaches to inspire both outreach and discipleship for today's church. Ray Simpson shows that such figures from past centuries can provide models for Christian life and witness today. He combines historical fact with spiritual lessons in a highly accessible style, with an appeal to a wide audience.

St Aidan's Way of Mission
Celtic insights for a post-Christian world
Ray Simpson
978 0 85746 485 9 £7.99

brfonline.org.uk

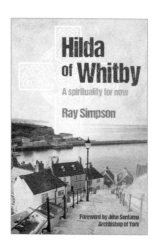

Born and reared among warring pagan tribes, through the influence of Celtic saints and scholars Hilda became a dominant figure in the development of the British Church, above all at the famous Synod where Celtic and Roman Churches came together. This book not only explores the drama of Hilda's life and ministry but shows what spiritual lessons we can draw for Christian life and leadership today.

Hilda of Whitby
A spirituality for now
Ray Simpson
978 1 84101 728 0 £7.99

brfonline.org.uk

If discipleship is about connecting more deeply with God and connecting God with the whole of life, Simon Reed argues, we're looking at a lifelong process that requires long-term skills rather than short-term courses. *Followers of the Way* explores how we can look to Celtic Christianity to inspire authentic Christian discipleship today.

Followers of the Way
Ancient discipleship for modern Christians
Simon Reed
978 1 80039 162 8 £9.99

brfonline.org.uk

Following the ancient rhythm of the Celtic year, these prayers, meditations and liturgies will help you focus on the natural flow of life as it changes around you. Based on the eight points of the Celtic year, each of the eight sections includes a liturgy for a full service, a week of daily readings, guided contemplations and a selection of prayers and blessings.

The Celtic Year
A rhythm of prayer and meditation for the eight points of the Celtic year
David Cole
978 0 85746 968 7 £8.99

brfonline.org.uk

 Ministries

Inspiring people of all ages to grow in Christian faith

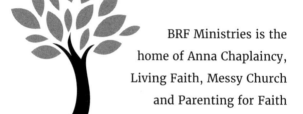

BRF Ministries is the home of Anna Chaplaincy, Living Faith, Messy Church and Parenting for Faith

As a charity, our work would not be possible without fundraising and gifts in wills.
To find out more and to donate,
visit brf.org.uk/give or call +44 (0)1235 462305